Fred Masters

Ye CANDLE MAKERS
Ye APOTHECARY

Ye
BLUSH
&
STUTTER

THE FIRST FLEET

Harvey, Roland, 1945-.
The first fleet.

ISBN 1 86388 709 1.

1. First Fleet, 1787-1788—Juvenile literature. 2. Convict Ships—Juvenile literature. 3. Voyages and travels—Juvenile literature. 4. Australia–History–To 1788—Juvenile literature. 5. Australia—Discovery and exploration—Juvenile literature. 6. New South Wales—History—To 1788—Juvenile literature.

A823.3

First published in 1982 by The Five Mile Press, Melbourne.
First published in paperback in 1983 by William Collins, Sydney.
This edition published in 1997 by Scholastic Australia Pty Limited ACN 000 614 577,
PO Box 579, Gosford 2250. Also in Sydney, Brisbane, Melbourne,
Adelaide and Perth. www.scholastic.com.au

Reprinted in 1998.

Printed and bound in China.

9 8 7 6 5 4 3 2 89 / 9

THE FIRST FLEET

ALAN BOARDMAN   ROLAND HARVEY

SCHOLASTIC
SYDNEY AUCKLAND NEW YORK TORONTO LONDON

YE APOTHECARY
ye
BLUSH AND
STUTTER

London 1783 – for many a city of poverty and despair. Food and shelter were scarce and expensive, few people had jobs and many were forced to steal in order to feed themselves and their families. The narrow, dirty streets were crowded with beggars, pickpockets and all manner of desperate men, women and children.

John Hudson, a chimney sweep from Middlesex, was arrested whilst breaking into a house to commit a burglary. He was sent for trial at the Old Bailey.

The penalty for burglary was death but because of his age, Hudson's sentence was reduced to seven years transportation. John Hudson was nine years old.

With British gaols filled to overflowing the government had, for a number of years, been transporting its unwanted criminals to America but with the 1776 War of Independence, that practice came to an end.

As the crime rate continued to rise the authorities were forced to use old ships as temporary prisons and it was in one of these that John Hudson was to spend the next three years of his life. On the River Thames over six hundred convicts were confined in this way – working ashore each day in chains and returning to the hulks each night.

INCREDIBLE

As time passed conditions aboard the hulks became unbearable. Convicts were given very little food, their drinking water – drawn from the river – was impure, and diseases began to spread out of control. In a little over two years more than 170 prisoners died.

Faced with this worsening situation the government decided, in 1786, to renew the system of transportation and elected to ship the convicts to Botany Bay. Sir Joseph Banks, the famous botanist who had travelled with James Cook on the *Endeavour* some years before, had spoken in glowing terms of this distant land and recommended the establishment of a British colony there.

John Hudson knew nothing of Botany Bay but as he was transferred from the prison ship to the transport *Friendship* early in 1787 he felt a certain optimism. Nothing, he was sure, could be as bad as the life he was leaving behind.

Portsmouth Harbour, where a total of eleven vessels were gathered together, was a scene of enormous activity. Convicts, huddled together in chains and under heavy guard, were brought from hulks and prisons all over England. Everywhere sailors, marines and civilians bustled about loading stores, checking equipment and making ready for the journey ahead.

Chosen to command this First Fleet was a retired naval officer Arthur Phillip, the son of a German teacher of languages and an English woman. Phillip had had previous experience in transporting convicts from Lisbon to Brazil when he served in the Portuguese navy and was regarded as a capable organiser and a good leader. He was appointed Governor of New South Wales and given the task of establishing a colony at Botany Bay.

In his charge were over 750 prisoners – men and women of all ages, and some very young children. Their crimes ranged from petty theft to highway robbery and murder.

After many delays the First Fleet slipped quietly out of Portsmouth at 5 o'clock on the morning of May 13th 1787 and began the long voyage to their new land. In addition to the convicts there were over 550 sailors, marines, officials, wives and children aboard the ships.

The fleet comprised six transports, three stores ships and two naval vessels – the *Sirius*, under the command of Governor Phillip, and the *Supply*.

Like many of the convicts John Hudson had never been to sea before and was not sure what to expect. At first it was all a great adventure – the sounds and smells of the ship were new and exciting but gradually excitement turned to boredom as one day followed another.

Below decks conditions were little better than on the hulks. Confined as they were in cramped spaces where the air was stale and where rats, cockroaches and bugs abounded the prisoners frequently fought amongst themselves. The worst offenders were flogged and placed in irons on the open decks.

They reached their first port of call, Tenerife in the Canary Islands, on June 3rd. For most of the prisoners it was their first glimpse of a foreign port.

The fleet remained at anchor in Santa Cruz harbour for a week taking on supplies of fresh meat, fruit and vegetables. By this time it was extremely hot and water rationing was introduced. In the ships, attempts were made to sweeten the air by the use of gunpowder explosions but all efforts to improve the ventilation failed and prisoners were continually fainting in the oppressive heat.

From Tenerife the fleet sailed for Rio de Janeiro and, catching favourable trade winds, reached that port in early August.

Here provisions were found to be moderately-priced and plentiful. Exotic fruits such as guavas, pineapples, coconuts and bananas, which many of the First Fleeters had never seen before, were readily available. To their delight the prisoners were allowed the run of the decks, under supervision, whilst the officers went ashore. They remained almost a month in Rio repairing sails, renewing food supplies, airing camping equipment and collecting a variety of plants and seeds they hoped to grow in the new colony.

Leaving Rio the fleet encountered some of the worst weather of the voyage as they crossed the South Atlantic ocean. Gale force winds whipped the seas into a frenzy and convicts and crew alike suffered terribly from sea-sickness. Huge waves crashed constantly over the decks drenching everyone aboard. With only one blanket each Hudson and his fellow convicts were continually racked with cold.

There were many occasions when even the most hardened sailors feared for their lives for anyone washed overboard would have no chance of surviving.

For those unused to the ways of the seas the noise and violent motion were terrifying in the extreme.

On October 13th they arrived at Table Bay at the Cape of Good Hope where they made good the damage caused by the heavy seas and took on additional livestock including horses, cattle, sheep, goats and chickens.

Leaving Table Bay in November the fleet set out on the last and longest leg of the journey. Anxious to make good time Governor Phillip transferred from *Sirius* to the faster ship *Supply* and with the transports *Alexander*, *Scarborough* and *Friendship* sailed ahead of the fleet.

In the middle of the Indian Ocean they spent their first Christmas Day away from England.

Seven weeks after leaving the Cape of Good Hope the advance party rounded Van Diemen's Land and on January 18th arrived at Botany Bay, a mere two days ahead of the rest of the fleet.

The land here appeared grim and inhospitable so, sailing even further north, Phillip discovered Port Jackson where the entire fleet anchored on January 26th, 1788. A landing party was sent ashore, and the British flag unfurled whilst the marines fired volleys into the air. Toasts were drunk to the health of the new colony.

Work began immediately on clearing the ground and within days tents were set up to house the officers, marines and convicts. Governor Phillip named the settlement Sydney in honour of the British Home Secretary.

The voyage had taken over eight months and covered about 24,000 kilometres. More than forty people had died since the fleet left England and seven babies had been born.

When he stepped ashore in New South Wales John Hudson was 13 years old.

As they settled down in their new surroundings Phillip and his men began to realise the enormity of the task ahead. Many of the convicts were too old to work whilst others were too sick or too lazy. The tools they brought from England proved inadequate for the harsh conditions, their plants and seeds failed to grow and wild dingoes made off with many of their sheep and poultry.

For over two years they struggled to survive on the remains of the stores they'd brought with them.

On June 3rd, 1790, with the new colony close to starvation and with many of the original convicts dead or seriously ill, the first ship of the second fleet, the *Lady Juliana*, sailed into Port Jackson with relief supplies and more convicts.

In 1791 John Hudson was given his freedom. He later received a grant of land and settled down to become a respected member of the community.

Ye CANDLE MAKERS
YE APOTHECARY

Ye BLUSH & STUTTER